Your journey into
The Stories from My Grandmother's Hands

STARTS HERE

This code gives you free access to an album of sounds and songs that will complement your experience of this book.

The Stories from My Grandmother's Hands

by

Dr. Resmaa Menakem and T. Mychael Rambo

Illustrations by Leroy Campbell

ISBN: 978-1-949481-94-5

Cover design: Jason Craft and Patti Frazee

Author photo of Resmaa Menakem by Bruce Silcox

Author photo of T. Mychael Rambo by Tom Wallace

Illustrator photo of Leroy Campbell by photographer/fine artist Maurice Evans

Black House Publishings
Minneapolis, MN
resmaa@resmaa.com

This book is dedicated to the memory of my friend, Christopher Sorensen,

and his children's children's children.

A Note from Resmaa

Thank you for taking this journey into *The Stories from My Grandmother's Hands*. This is more than a children's book. It is an interactive experience to be shared between generations. It is a toybox to help children create joy and manage the energetics of white-body supremacy.

If your child has a Black body or a body of culture, the five toys of cultural somatics in this book will help them address different forms of racialized trauma (historical, intergenerational, persistent institutional and personal). In *The Stories from My Grandmother's Hands*, children will gently learn to play with these toys, along with their parents and caregivers. By doing these practices together, children learn that they and their people are not defective. Things happened to their people before they got here.

If your child has a white body, this book will give them and you a space to discuss white-body supremacy in a way that can de-center the white body as standard, and will temper the activation stress response in white children and their caregivers. This may help with the cultivation of embodied antiracist practices in the white community between generations.

The accompanying soundtrack includes white and brown noises to aid in rest and discernment. You can learn more about this soundtrack and other opportunities for engagement by visiting TheStoriesFromMyGrandmothersHands.com.

You will see different names for "grandmother" represented in this book. We have added footnotes to inform you where the names originated.

Again, thank you for taking this journey. Together we can start to build an embodied antiracist culture.

— Resmaa

My grandmother's hands are big like sunrise, with fingers thick and coarse, like the cornrows braided into her silver-grey hair.

My grandmother's hands picked cotton.

My Granny's hands rest on her belly
as she hums and sighs, rocks and sways,
like leaves swirling in the breeze.

My grandmother's hands left handprints on my heart.

My Big Mama's hands cook collard greens, macaroni and cheese, and fried chicken, and make pitchers of fresh-squeezed lemonade.

My grandmother's hands sure could cook.

My Abuela's* hands turn the pages of books that lull me to sleep with stories of far-off lands and magical kingdoms.

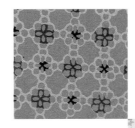

*Spain/Morocco/Latin America

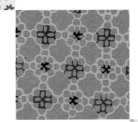

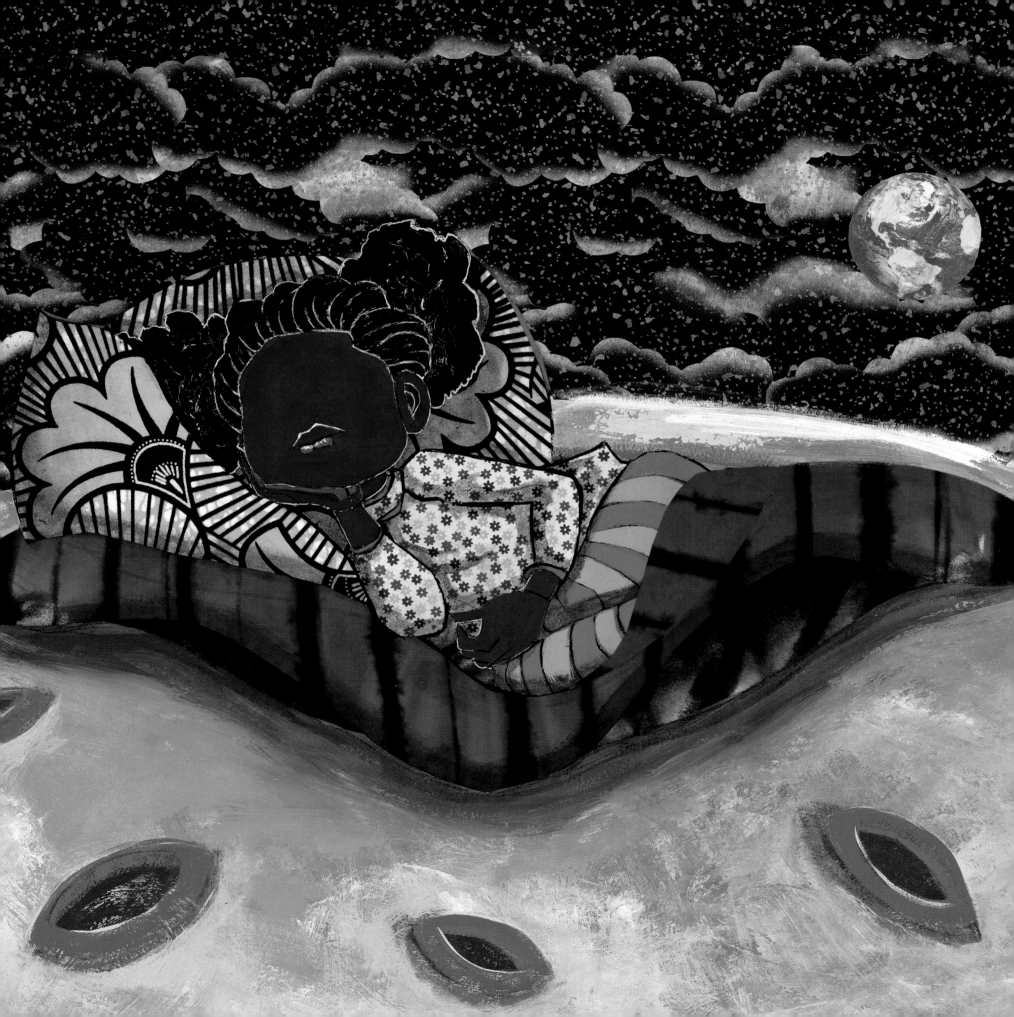

My grandmother's hands taught me to dream big!

My Gee Gee's hands type beautiful messages, send heartfelt well wishes, and place stamps with brown faces on cards to family and friends.

Love
geegee

My grandmother's hands
held memories.

My Avo's* hands cradle my face, pinch my cheeks, and make me smile out loud.

*Brazilian/Portuguese

My grandmother's hands brought me joy.

My Oma's* hands snap and clap, brushing against one another, while she taps her feet and laughs like fireworks.

*South African/Afrikaans/Dutch
(Zulu = Ugogo or Gogo)

Thank you for sharing this special day, my 90th Birthday, with me!

My grandmother's hands made music.

My Nana's* hands push and pull, glide, and guide me down curvy sidewalks toward spaces where I can pause and be still.

*Nigerian/British (Nigerian/Hausas = Ka-ka-N-ta)

My grandmother's hands showed me
how to soothe my soul.

My Grann's* hands make shadow puppets and finger paint gardens of colorful flowers.

*Haitian Creole/French

My grandmother's hands were creative.

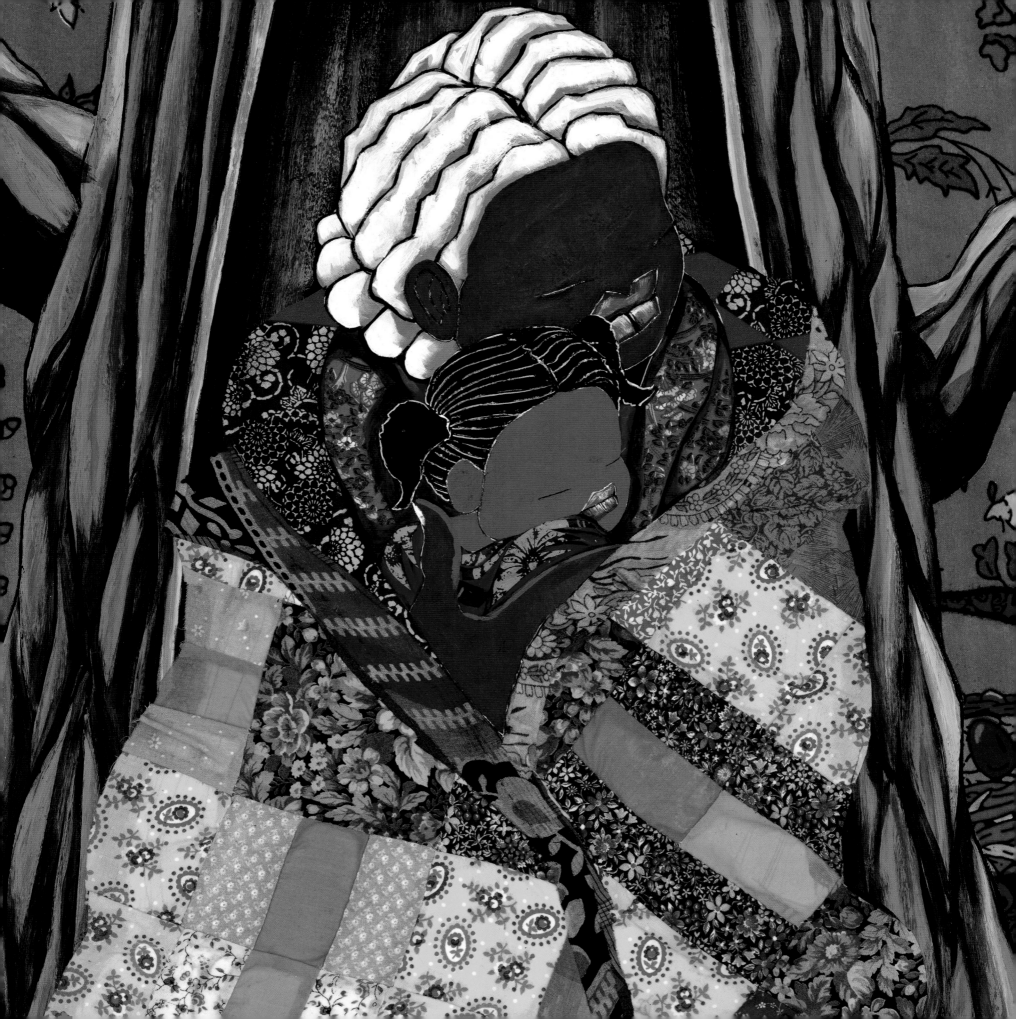

My Gramma's hands wrap me up in a blanket of love and plant me in the now, like a deeply rooted tree.

My grandmother's hands always reminded me to breathe.

Learn More

To learn more about this book and the use of the five somatic toys, visit TheStoriesFromMyGrandmothersHands.com/how-to/

Please use the WYSER app to deepen your sense of understanding and embodiment. You will be connected to videos and other resources that help you embody the teachings. This process is called somatic elicitation, where we learn to temper and condition our bodies through small pieces of racialized exposure. You can find the WYSER app by using this QR code, by going to your Android or Apple app store, or at the web address below:
https://wyserapp.com/

If you're interested in going deeper into the ideas of Somatic Abolitionism, join the community at https://blackoctopussociety.com/

About the Collaborators

Dr. Resmaa Menakem is a healer, a longtime therapist, and a licensed clinical social worker who specializes in the healing of racialized trauma. He is also the founder of the Cultural Somatics Institute, a cultural trauma navigator, and a communal provocateur and coach. Resmaa is best known as the author of the *New York Times* bestseller *My Grandmother's Hands: Racialized Trauma and the Pathway to Mending Our Hearts and Bodies*, and as the originator and key advocate of Somatic Abolitionism, an embodied antiracist practice of living and culture building. He received an Honorary Doctorate of Humane Letters in Social Justice, Somatic Education and Advocacy from the California Institute of Integral Studies.

For ten years, Resmaa cohosted a radio show with former U.S. Congressman Keith Ellison on KMOJ-FM in Minneapolis. He also hosted his own show, *Resmaa in the Morning*, on KMOJ. Resmaa has appeared on both *The Oprah Winfrey Show* and *Dr. Phil* as an expert on family dynamics, couples in conflict, and domestic violence. He has also been a guest on Charlamagne Tha God's Comedy Central TV program, *Tha God's Honest Truth*, and on iHeart radio's *The Breakfast Club* with DJ Envy and *Way Up with Angela Yee*.

T. Mychael Rambo is a three-time regional Emmy Award-winning actor, vocalist, arts educator, and community organizer. He has made an indelible mark in the Twin Cities, performing principal roles at such theaters as Penumbra, the Guthrie, the Ordway, Illusion Theatre, Mixed Blood, Park Square Theatre, Children's Theatre, and Minnesota Opera, to name but a few. Nationally and internationally, his stage credits include Carnegie Hall and performances abroad in Africa, Europe, and South America. He has appeared in local and national television commercials, feature films, HBO mini-series, and other television programming. T. Mychael is an accomplished recording artist (with two acclaimed recordings under his belt), a K-12 residency artist, and an affiliate professor in the College of Liberal Arts, Theatre Arts and Dance at the University of Minnesota, as well as a highly sought-after public speaker and committed community organizer.

Leroy Campbell is a master gardener, painter, storyteller, author, public speaker, illustrator, and lover of souls. He paints a beautiful hope for humanity through his art and through his words. In telling the stories he knows best, he is offering the wisdom and lessons of the elders as a gift to us all. His paintings, infused with history, tie the past to the present in the practice of sankofa, the understanding that you can't move forward until you receive the lessons of the past. The vulnerability of his art, his soul, his ability to tell a story through the use of acrylic, paper, tapestries, and organic materials, create an opportunity for conversation, for something real, for the human connection that we are all desperately seeking.